FOX-NAHEM

FOX-NAHEM

The Design Vision of Joe Nahem

Anthony Iannacci

Foreword by Robert Downey Jr.

ABRAMS, NEW YORK

This book is dedicated to my partner
Jeffrey Fields, Tom Fox, my family,
our clients, and the Fox-Nahem team.
I am forever grateful.

—Joe Nahem

Contents

Foreword

Why am I writing an intro to a design book? Read on—

A few summers ago, my wife Susan and I were looking for a summer rental in the Hamptons. We must have viewed at least seventy-five properties, many of which boasted top-drawer designers and the like, but there was a clear standout: Joe Nahem and his partner Jeff's Amagansett home. From the overall layout and flow of the home to the small details, like the kitchen table and chairs (which reminded me of the lobby bar at Paris's L'Hotel), it had the vibe of an inviting, sophisticated, and curated space. Joe had clearly put much thought into how folks live, eat, congregate, and chill in their homes. We rented the place, and our kids had a blast; too many relatives visited, and many fond memories were made.

That could've been the end of the story, but the Mrs. said, "We have to meet them. They'd have great ideas for our new place out West." I called Joe to see if we could have lunch before the lease expired. By the time our salad plates were cleared, we were old pals. We now have two exciting projects with Fox-Nahem: one is a modern Binishell in Malibu, the other is a classic Windmill estate in East Hampton (acquired partly due to Joe's "strong recommend," let's say).

Our previous experience with designers was sucky. We'd pretty much surrender to the *will of the experts*, then harbor a white-hot resentment. Nothing was within budget, it wasn't actually collaborative, and the pressure allowed for little levity.

Designing your home is supposed to be fun, but it needs to get *done*. Enter Joe—aka "force of nature"—Nahem. He is calm and available, curious and confident, always playing with new materials, shapes, colors, and textiles, while exhaustively cultivating relationships with emerging artisans.

When necessary, he employs Jedi mind tricks, smirks, frowns, eye-rolls, or impassioned pleas, and if all else fails, Joe will allow us our occasional folly. Yet, Mrs. Downey and I have enjoyed a remarkable collaboration with the entire Fox-Nahem team. We've been pushed out of our "comfort zone" without losing our personal sense of style, taste, or dignity. Joe is almost always right in his design decisions without being unreasonable or smarmy. It's been an education to say the least.

The proof, however, is in yonder pudding. What follows is a heaping tablespoon of it. So, I guess I'm writing this opener because I suspect our several Fox-Nahem projects might make it into the *next* book. Maybe you'll write the intro to *that* one?

—Robert Downey Jr.

Introduction

Sometimes, not often, the worlds of art, fashion, architecture, and interior design overlap. When this occurs, we tend to see it in the similarities of the physical manifestations. Alexander McQueen's obsessive attention to details, the whimsical collage quality of Tony Duquette, or the minimalist appeal of John Pawson all carry direct, formal associations to the world of fine art and artists. But what if we were to consider the notion of a shared strategy among creative disciplines and not limit our understanding of the work to the similarities of the physical manifestations? Can an interior designer, for example, play with signification, a strategy more commonly associated with today's art world than with that of decoration? What would that look like, and how would we "read" it?

I started to ask myself this question as I was working with Joe Nahem and his partner Jeff Fields on this book. Yes, many of the homes Joe has designed, which I am very proud to present here, host important works of contemporary art, but they are just as likely to host handcrafted custom furnishings or complex architectural details of Joe's design, as well as bespoke fabrics, textiles, and finishes by other artisans.

As this collection of Joe's work was coming together, I noticed that somehow he was doing more than installing blue-chip works of contemporary art adjacent to exquisite antique, vintage, and new furnishings. It occurred to me that on many occasions the manner in which those works were installed, how they relate to the surroundings Joe has created for them, and, therefore, the context within which we perceive them actually changed how I was reading both the works of art and the environments Joe had created. Somehow the distinctions between decorator and curator were merging together. The term "decorator," I discovered, describes the individual charged with the task of making something look more attractive by adding extra items or images to it. A "curator," on the other hand, is defined as a manager or overseer of a cultural institution; a content specialist charged with an institution's collections and involved with the interpretation of such material.

With these definitions in mind, Joe's work started to reveal interesting strategies. To draw a comparison between the private homes featured here and cultural heritage institutions may seem like a stretch, but when the artwork and many of the objects Joe incorporates into these designs are, for lack of a better term, of "museum quality," the comparison holds up. The fact that highly recognized architects who were also known to design cultural institutions, from Stanford White to Annabelle Selldorf, designed many of these homes simply underscores the possibility.

Perhaps this strategy is best seen in the entry foyer of the 1920s-era Park Avenue duplex Joe designed for a couple with a passion for provocative contemporary art. When writing about design I always try to avoid the backstory. After all, it's the images of beautifully appointed spaces that people want to see and learn from, right? But the fact that Jacqueline Kennedy's grandfather developed this building and that she actually grew up in this apartment has a bearing on Joe's design. Now, one might expect that he would have designed a nostalgic tribute to this iconic maven of style and supporter of American excellence in design, and that it is therefore important that we understand Jacqueline's relationship to the space, but with the help of Jeff Koons, his clients, and their art consultant, Joe plays with that expectation and uses it to create context and significance. Visitors to the home are greeted by two pieces by Koons: a pair of Yorkshire terriers, a sculptural piece in polychromed wood that sits atop a mid-century Italian entry table, and his "New Hoover Deluxe Shampoo Polishers," three identical domestic appliances in an acrylic case with fluorescent lights. This is not what one would expect to encounter upon entering the childhood home of one of America's most-loved first ladies. The contrast between the art and the expectations the space carries sets the tone for the entire duplex.

Moments like this make it clear that what Joe is doing goes beyond the role of decorator as enlightened shopper. It flirts with the notion of interior design as a means to not only exalt the beauty of a collection of furnishings and art, but also to enhance the significance of those objects by directing a reading and understanding of them.

In the dining room of a Hamptons weekend retreat, for example, he hung an impressive Kara Walker cut-paper work, a silhouette of a female character, over a mid-century Brazilian credenza, which is paired with a dining table with the same provenance and plantation-style chairs, all atop a patchwork cowhide rug. Joe has a basic knowledge of Walker's work, which very directly addresses issues of racism, sexism, colonialism, and slavery, and his assemblage of art and furnishings in this dining room clearly calls to mind a stylish Brazilian ranch, and underscores Walker's dialogue on colonialism and slavery through a conscious lens of privilege.

Joe plays with juxtapositions of art, furnishings, and function to create tension and interest in many of his projects, and these combinations often elevate both the art and the interior design. But Joe is just as likely to elevate the work of the craftsmen and women he is fond of working with as he is to enhance an interpretation of the artwork he has the privilege to incorporate into his projects.

In the two-and-a-half-story living room of a Greenwich Village townhouse, constructed in the 1800s and then altered by Paul Rudolph and later by Steven Harris, Joe installed a sculptural artwork by Spencer Finch. Finch's work, entitled "Thirty Brightest Stars in the Milky Way," is composed of thirty glass globes, each fitted with an electric bulb and each intended to represent a specific star. The globes are of differing sizes and colors and hung at varying heights. The color Finch uses on each of the globes refers to the wavelength of light the star emits; the size of each globe references the size of each star; and the height at which it was hung was determined by the star's distance from earth. Finch's installation invites an upward gaze both physically and conceptually, but it also sets a standard of meaning. There is nothing random or haphazard about Finch's work, and Joe follows Finch's lead and carries a level of significance into his choices as well. On the mantel breast Joe incorporated a custom, low-luster plaster finish that goes from dark to light gray as it moves toward the ceiling and approaches the hanging Finch artwork. The gesture not only provides Finch's work with abundant white space near the ceiling, but also directs our attention to it in a beautiful and subtle way.

Unlike a traditional curator, Joe is not simply an outsider pulling together the work of others. He is fond of antiques and vintage furnishings, but explains that when new production is as expensive as custom, he will always go for custom and finds great joy and dynamic results in the process of designing specifically for his projects. Joe does not limit his custom designs to sofas and dining tables. On the following pages you will see everything from fire breasts composed of thousands of metal rods to undulating walls in free-form Corian of Joe's design. And it seems as if every time Joe moves toward the custom, it is in an effort to exalt an important work of art, furniture, or craft, yet still maintain a comfortable and inviting living environment for his clients.

Joe is inspired by the art he is working with and some of his formal decisions appear to be drawn from the same inspirational pool that artists often dip into. All good designers understand the formal notion of contrast—dark and light, hard and soft—and Joe certainly applies those concepts to his work. In one such project, a penthouse loft, he applies this simple idea of contrast to exalt a collection of furnishings while providing the living room with a unique identity. Joe felt as if the ever-present grid of windows here provided the space with an abundance of square geometry. To counter this, nearly everything he brought into the room, with the exception of a custom dining table, embraces the curvilinear—from the settee by Chantal Saccomanno and Olivier Dayot to the custom rug, which Joe designed with a wild serpentine edge.

Joe has been designing highly functioning, comfortable interiors for years and has had much success along the way, but that has never caused him to become static or formulaic. In fact, his success has had the opposite effect on his work. Like a good curator, Joe juxtaposes objects, furnishings, finishes, and art, moving beyond pleasing and functional combinations, and opening chains of significance that enhance not only meaning and understanding, but beauty. With each new project he grows more creative and more confident. Joe inspires craftspeople and derives great satisfaction from pushing them, as he does himself, to explore their craft. As I have followed Joe's work over the years, I have seen him mature and become more confident. That confidence is contagious. You feel it the moment you walk into one of the spaces he has designed.

—Anthony Iannacci

Greenwich Village Townhouse

The thought of a landmarked Greenwich Village townhouse on a tree-lined street conjures up expectations of grand parlors, original moldings, mantels, stair rails, and banisters: luxurious places where inhabitants live with a constant reminder of the city's gaslight-era past. During the mid–twentieth century the city established landmark districts, which prohibited owners of buildings in those areas from altering their street-side facades. Despite their carefully preserved exteriors, many of these iconic structures offer a world of surprise on their interiors; this is one such home.

The current owners were initially drawn to the building because, once inside, it defied all expectations of historic living. In the 1970s, the renowned modernist architect Paul Rudolph seriously altered the home's interior spaces by removing the back wall and replacing it with a two-and-a-half-story grid of windows looking onto the rear garden. The owners, fans of Rudolph's work and active collectors of contemporary art, were taken by the building's modernist pedigree and hoped to maintain as much of Rudolph's gesture as possible, but they also required additional square footage.

In order to achieve these goals, the owners hired the architect Steven Harris and the interior designer Joe Nahem. Harris, along with his project architect John Woell, quickly understood that the Rudolph renovation needed to be completely rebuilt and developed—a plan that would create additional space by both excavating below grade and building up. Harris and his team also restored the building's original front stoop, which had been removed to create more usable space on the parlor floor, diverting all egress through the existing English basement.

By returning the building's original entrance to the parlor floor, Harris reestablished the circulation of this floor to its initial design. However, this meant moving the dining room downstairs for additional space, and adding a full basement, incorporating the gym, spa, and dining room beneath the English basement, where the kitchen and den are located.

There is something almost Alice in Wonderland–like about walking up the stoop, entering the vestibule and then the entry gallery, which both maintain their early-1800s proportions, and then seeing the main circulation stairwell and the living room beyond with its soaring ceilings and wall of glass. It is as if one is thrust from the early 1800s to the present just by entering the space.

Nahem underscores this shift in scale by using a variety of surface materials, colors, and textures. The intimate spaces, like the master bedroom, are more in keeping with the scale and proportions of the original historic structure and are more "decorated" in a 360-degree sense, while the very contemporary vast light-filled living room maintains a white, loft-like feeling that bleeds into the public areas.

Nahem acknowledges that art collectors like these clients can propose specific challenges: They often desire large, properly illuminated walls, but here he wanted to design a home that did not look or feel like a museum. His goal was to create a space rich in color, texture, and form in which those attributes were not limited to the artworks. Thus, many of the fabrics used in the home, like that on the sofa in the living room, are either handmade or hand-altered, connecting them to the artwork throughout the house. The varied textures and fabrics add contrast and functionality to this home and heighten the tension between those elements that clearly recall the early 1800s proportions and the more contemporary spaces.

In the entry vestibule, Nahem installed an antique reclaimed marble floor from Paris Ceramics and hung David Wiseman lighting and a photograph by Richard Prince.

Beyond the foyer, an ample entry space is used as a gallery. Here, artworks by Roberto Cuoghi, Michelle Grabner, and Mickalene Thomas are installed. The artist Marilyn Minter designed the rug.

Both Nahem and Harris wanted to preserve the transparency of the two-and-a-half-story wall of glass in the living room. To do so, Nahem installed sheer curtains, producing a warm, welcoming environment. The room features two Fox-Nahem custom swivel chairs with fabric woven by Toyine Sellers. Woven leather was also used on a suite of Swedish chairs by Kerstin Hörlin-Holmquist at the game table, which was designed by the Fox-Nahem team. Hanging above the fireplace is a painting by Ross Bleckner.

Above: Sitting atop the game table is a bust by Simone Leigh. The space also features a tapestry by Gabriel Kuri and a painting by Al Taylor.

Left: The living room rug by Jan Kath morphs as it moves through the space. Inspired by a traditional Turkish rug, Nahem custom-tailored the pattern so that in some areas it is very evident and in others it nearly fades into one color. Nahem also designed the curvilinear sofa with the hopes that it would ground the lofty space. The colors were chosen to complement the commissioned Spencer Finch installation of colored glass hanging above; for a touch of texture, the back of the sofa was hand-outline quilted.

Above: Nahem installed a hanging cabinet by Paul Evans in the hallway leading into the den, and placed Carlo Bugatti chairs on either side. The artwork directly above is by Huma Bhabha.

Right: A space for casual meals, the den features a custom banquette by Fox-Nahem, which sits below a piece by Sergej Jensen. Outside in the back garden is a sculpture by Nick van Woert.

The newly created lower level, which extends from the street to the back of the property line, includes the dining room, gym, spa area, and wine cellar. Harris suspended the back garden above the newly excavated space with light wells and plantings along the perimeter. For the dining room, Nahem and his team designed the walnut and inlaid brass table; the chairs are vintage Josef Frank. The room also includes artwork by Candida Höfer and Vik Muniz.

Above: A wool and silk hand-knotted rug from Martin Patrick Evan creates a backdrop in the den. Here, both the sofa and ottoman are custom Fox-Nahem designs. The ottoman is made from cowhide and features a bronze plate. On the wall, Nahem installed a set of album covers designed by Gary Simmons.

Opposite: In the hallway, a vintage Scandinavian Märta Måås-Fjetterström rug from Nazmiyal shares the space with a Carlo Bugatti chair and a sculpture, which appears to sprout out from between the wall and floor, by Tony Matelli. The photograph hanging directly above is by Paul Pfeiffer.

For the master bath, which runs the entire width of the building and includes three original windows, Nahem clad some of the walls in limestone and intricately carved Moroccan plaster. The bath fittings are by Waterworks, and the stool below the sink is by the Haas Brothers. Artwork by Elad Lassry hangs on the wall above the bathtub.

Nahem incorporates upholstered walls in this very intimately scaled master bedroom. Here, the horizontal pattern used on the wall seamlessly transforms into the upholstered headboard. In this monochromatic space, Nahem relies on the play of texture to create interest and variation. The highly textured carpet by Rosemary Hallgarten creates a welcome contrast to the finer fabrics used on the walls and for the window treatments. The bedside tables are a custom design by Fox-Nahem.

Oceanfront Family Home

Nahem's clients purchased this 1970s-era beach house for both its size and scale and its commanding location. While the original structure was inspired by modernist architecture, it did not possess the kind of architectural attributes or pedigree that would cause one to hesitate before making major changes. Because the structure offered ocean views on one side and bay views on the other, both of which are best appreciated from the second story, the house was originally designed with the public spaces on the upper floor and the bulk of the bedrooms, with the exception of the master, on the ground floor. Nahem maintained this "upside-down" organization, but efforts were made to render it less awkward.

Nahem worked on the house in two distinct phases. The first phase included transforming the cramped entry into a soaring two-story foyer, decorating the interiors, and redesigning the original bathrooms. By incorporating the stairway, the foyer renovation provided visual access to the upper floor and helped mitigate the separation between the ground-floor entry and the second-story living spaces. The reclaimed antique limestone with a heavy patina used on the floors further distinguishes the entry from the rest of the house, where Nahem used reclaimed oak.

In a second intervention, Nahem worked with the architect Steve Chrostowski of Alveary Architecture to create an addition that would host a great room, family room, kitchen, dining room, and guest bedrooms. Nahem and Chrostowski were careful to take the right cues from the original structure. Their goal was to increase the size of the home while substantially enhancing the appeal of its original modernist inspiration. Standard, typically suburban materials were upgraded with custom, natural ones. The windows, for example, were replaced with more ample, mahogany-framed fenestrations, and a hand-split cedar roof was substituted for the sea of typical composite material. On the interior, reclaimed or painted paneling on walls and ceilings was favored over Sheetrock wherever possible.

Nahem, along with architect Brian O'Keefe, had very successfully added the heroic entry during the first phase of work. In the second he continued down this path with oversized public rooms. His clients wanted space to install some of the larger artworks in their collection, and Nahem also felt that the open vistas the site provided should be reflected in ample, airy interior spaces.

In order to accommodate some of the oversized art, a number of large walls were left free, and in some spaces, the designer and architect increased the ceiling height to host specific artworks. Furniture was also a consideration. In the dining room, for example, Nahem designed a server that hovers above the floor and away from the walls, leaving the vertical spaces free for art, like a painting by Richard Prince.

Because the scale of these rooms can be the antithesis of intimate and personal, Nahem was careful to choose materials and colors for their warmth and textural interest. The great room is a clear example of this. A "conversation pit" was added to distinguish this room from the more formal living room, and to enhance the notion of warmth while creating an inviting space.

In some of the spaces—the dining room, for example—the large-scale art takes on a commanding position. In other rooms, such as the great room with its fireplace wall or the kitchen with its table and banquette, Nahem's work becomes the source of creative spark. While Nahem and his team's creations are custom and unique, they are not intended to compete with the art or views, but instead to create a warm and inviting living environment. Therefore, he was careful to keep his expressions monochromatic and utilitarian.

The entry features back-painted glass doors and stair risers. Hanging along the stairs are two oversized works of art: "Apple" by Nate Lowman and a mirror mosaic by Jim Hodges.

Large corner windows were incorporated into the great room to provide open views of the water. The bar, custom designed by Nahem, is made from similar materials to those used for the fireplace, and helps complete the room. Nahem added vintage "Lions in Frost" lucite stools to the bar area, along with vintage chairs by Pierre Paulin.

Following spread: Comfort and practicality were the primary concerns for Nahem in the great room. Reclaimed barn wood is applied in a modern fashion to the vaulted ceiling to provide the space with a sense of warmth and intimacy, and a monumental, sunken conversation pit was designed by Nahem to be as welcoming and comfortable as possible. The fireplace surround is a custom Nahem design composed of hundreds of metal rods welded together like a sea of pick-up sticks. Artwork by Ed Ruscha and Walton Ford hangs in the room.

Right: Marilyn Minter's 2009 "Pretty/Dirty" hangs in the dining room and contributes to the celebration of scale that is part of each room of this home.

Previous spread: For the dining room, Nahem commissioned artist Jeff Zimmerman to create a chandelier composed of iridescent glass balls. Mira Nakashima, George Nakashima's daughter, with whom Nahem has often collaborated, designed an oversized table that could comfortably host up to sixteen guests. Hanging at one end of the table is a painting by Walton Ford.

Above: The upper cabinets, a combination of mirror-finish stainless steel and glass, were designed by Nahem and made by Poggenpohl. The transparency and reflective quality of the cabinetry frees the visual pathway to the ocean beyond while still providing some storage.

Left: The kitchen, designed by Nahem and Fox-Nahem associate David Gorman, hosts an impressive table and banquette, two pieces that Nahem designed and had constructed in thermal-molded Corian with leather cushions on the seating surfaces. These sculptural furnishings occupy an inviting spot below a corner window with a commanding view. Hanging above the chrome cart is a piece by John Baldessari.

West Village Townhouse

Newly constructed townhomes are rare in Manhattan. With land costs among the highest in the world, the building type often falls under the responsibility of historic preservationists rather than developers. But in 2009 the architect Robert Stern, known for his interest in historic building types, was commissioned to add a fifty-three-unit high-rise and seven one-of-a-kind townhomes to a riverfront West Village location just beyond the limits of the area's historic district. Stern made great efforts to infuse the buildings with a sense of history and tie them not only to the neighborhood's protected early nineteenth-century buildings, but also to the city's long-standing love affair with such historic single-family homes. At the same time, he provided occupants with modern amenities luxury contemporary buyers expect.

The owners of this home were drawn to the single-family structure and appreciated Stern's nostalgic vision, but they also wanted the interior spaces to more accurately reflect their contemporary style and interest in provocative yet playful contemporary art. They turned to Joe Nahem to create an interior that would celebrate the tension between Stern's design, firmly grounded in an appreciation for the past, and their interest in vibrant contemporary culture, art, and decoration.

Nahem and his team felt that the floor plan, scale, and proportion of most of the rooms would suit his clients' needs. Many of the more challenging problems to solve with historic townhomes had already been considered by Stern's office; however, Nahem felt that the entry needed to be enlarged. He also wanted this introductory space to communicate that his intervention here was not about re-creating the past, or even referring to the building's imagined past. Instead Nahem's design called for wrapping the walls in undulating, free-form white Corian. The result is both simple and beautiful, and the highly unexpected monochromatic envelope not only sets the tone when one enters the home, but also focuses one's attention on some of the clients' smaller works of art.

With the bulk of the rooms left as they were constructed, Nahem concentrated his efforts on texture, surface, form, and color. Much of the house was designed around the clients' art collection, which has a particularly playful slant. In the entry-level living room, the walls are painted in a high-gloss white lacquer. Nahem designed the fireplace, which occupies the opposite wall, using a combination of free-form black Corian and smoked glass. One playful piece brought in by Nahem was the living room's custom sofa, which has a free-form sheared mink cape. Nahem continues this lively, nearly ironic reflection of his clients' art collection with whimsical gold-plated fittings in the bright-red powder room.

The family room is located on the lower level and provides direct access to the back garden. In this space, Nahem creates a certain tension with unexpected combinations of details and materials. He covered the walls in horizontal knotty pine paneling, which was then whitewashed, and designed a fireplace mantel breast that incorporates a combination of white Corian and metal mesh inset panels. Nahem also used his boldest upholstery colors to both enliven and brighten the space within the English basement, rendering it more casual.

In contrast to the bold colors and details of the powder room, the master bedroom continues the subtle play of pale gray, beige, and purple hues that were introduced in the living room. Much of the clients' art collection invites a sense of wonder, and Nahem underscores that at every opportunity, from the undulating white Corian walls of the entry to the custom upholstery in bold form or color.

The entry space walls are wrapped in undulating, free-form white Corian, creating a clean slate for artwork, like the Damien Hirst hanging past the doorframe.

The textured rug, custom designed by Nahem and made by Sacco Carpet, is the backdrop for an eclectic mix of objects in the formal living room, including a playful sculpture by the artist Hyungkoo Lee. This piece, a painstakingly accurate depiction of what appears to be the skeleton of the beloved animated character Goofy, sits before an overscale work by Gilbert & George. Vintage metal and upholstered chairs by Jules Leleu surround the game table.

The unfinished drape of the sofa was a deliberate decision by Nahem. When the designer was visiting his upholsterer's shop, he was shown the mink detail as a work in progress; the pelts had been applied, but not trimmed. Nahem decided on the spot that the unfinished drape would actually make for a very playful detail for the living room. Paired with the sofa are side chairs by Paul Evans and a ring coffee table by Mattia Bonetti and Élizabeth Garouste.

Right: The room also hosts a custom fire surround, which Nahem designed in mirror and free-form Corian. The monolithic element reflects light into the space and provides a whimsical contrast to the pair of eighteenth-century fruitwood and pine Italian console tables. Hanging directly above each table are artworks by Jim Lambie.

The den, on the lower level, which provides direct access to the rear garden, hosts a bar alcove and dining area. Here, Nahem combined crisp cabinetry with a reflective backsplash made from a custom-designed artisan glass. The table is by George Nakashima, and sits between bookcases by Edward Wormley.

Above: The powder room's walls are lacquered in a deep coral color. The mirror above the sink is vintage 1940s French.

Right: In the living room, Fox-Nahem lined the walls with white-washed knotty pine. A pair of Milo Baughman swivel chairs from the 1970s and a custom Fox-Nahem–designed sofa sits atop a custom Moroccan rug from ALT for Living.

The master bedroom was designed to function as a relaxing oasis. Here, upholstered panels extend across the headboard wall and become part of the structure of the bed. The upholstery both softens the environment and renders it more cocoon-like. The palette in this room has been limited to pale grays and dusty violets in an attempt to underscore the calming aspects of the space.

Weekend Retreat

After successfully designing his clients' Manhattan duplex, Joe Nahem was commissioned to update the family's Long Island retreat. The traditional twentieth-century shingled house required some changes: The owners longed for a larger master bedroom, home offices for each of them, bedrooms for their now-adult children, and a larger family room. The original structure was built around a two-story step-down living room and mezzanine with a wing on either side. Nahem found the proportions of the soaring living room unwelcoming. His unconventional proposal called for lowering the living room ceiling to a luxurious twelve feet and using the newly created space above for the couple's master suite. In addition, one of the wings was demolished and rebuilt to host a den leading to a screened-in porch with expanded bedrooms on the floor above. The opposing wing was extended to make room for a new kitchen and enlarged family room. Due to these extensive architectural alterations, Nahem worked closely with his longtime collaborators at Alveary Architecture.

In addition to increasing the size of the home, Nahem's goal was to provide each room with a distinct identity, an idea that evolved as the rooms came together. He installed reclaimed oak on many of the floors and avoided Sheetrock wherever possible. The walls in the den, for example, were clad in whitewashed knotty pine, while the ceiling featured clear pine that was then painted. The master bedroom ceiling was constructed from reclaimed barn wood and the den walls were made from cork. Teak along with Corian was used in the master bath, while the living room and dining room featured painted plaster.

While Nahem included a wide array of materials in the rooms, he largely limited his use of color and pattern to the rugs and upholstery. Throughout the house Nahem incorporated juxtapositions of color, texture, furnishings, and art. This created tension and contrast between the individual elements, further enhancing their interest and beauty. In the light-filled living room, for example, Nahem left the walls white, but installed a custom rug of an intricate green, yellow, and white pattern. The rug fills the room with a sense of the organic outdoor spaces beyond the windows and appears to breathe life into the once-unwelcoming space.

In the dining room, Nahem acts more like a curator than decorator. He painted the plaster walls a pale sage, and installed a massive mid-century dining table by the Brazilian designer Sérgio Rodrigues, his clients' set of rustic nineteenth-century dining chairs, and a rug by Martin Patrick Evan composed of a patchwork of cowhides. A blown-glass chandelier of dynamic, organic shapes by Jeff Zimmerman hangs above Nahem's unexpected arrangement and provides the room with a sense of wonder. To further expand on this notion of the whimsical, Nahem installed a black cut-paper silhouette by the artist Kara Walker. Her work explores issues of race, gender, and history, and it appears as if Nahem has created a surreal theatrical context as it interacts with the other furnishings. The resulting tension is beautiful and thought-provoking.

Nahem knew his clients were not interested in excessive or useless items, and as a consequence, many of the rooms have a nearly minimalist feel without ever feeling sparse or uninviting. Nahem accomplishes this by concentrating his efforts in unexpected areas. For example, the foyer and living room rugs provide the main source of color in those spaces; the kitchen, den, and family room feature furniture that provides a pop of bright color and acts as a backdrop for the custom-designed elements of the home. In every room, the sum is always greater than the parts.

In the entry foyer and living room beyond, Nahem relied on exuberantly colored rugs to provide the space with a chromatic identity. This allowed him to leave the walls neutral and still create spaces with strong identities. Hanging on one wall of the foyer is a painting by Joel Shapiro, which complements the colorful Jan Kath rug.

In the living room, bright white walls, a partial glass ceiling at the far end, and the large paned window provide the environment with the light-filled feeling of a conservatory. The rug by Fedora Designs, which is a custom Nahem design of various greens and yellows, reads like a welcoming meadow or a vast indoor lawn, and brings the verdant garden beyond the window into the space. The settee sitting atop the rug is by Robsjohn-Gibbings. Providing another pop of color to the room is a painting by José Parlá.

Above: A mid-century Italian game table with custom woven upholstery by Toyine Sellers occupies a corner of the living room. Nahem likes to incorporate game tables whenever he can, as he believes that such pieces extend the uses of contemporary living spaces.

Opposite: The furnishings, including this custom sofa of Nahem and associate David Gorman's design, maintain a light, airy quality that furthers the play on indoors versus outdoors.

A cut-paper work by Kara Walker hangs in the dining room above a Brazilian mid-century credenza. The room also features a mid-century Sérgio Rodrigues table and a blown-glass chandelier by Jeff Zimmerman, both from R & Company.

Above: Nahem designed the kitchen with a neutral palette, and added personalized details to the space, like the cabinets. The Corian island, designed by Nahem and made by Associated Fabrication, features custom crenellation.

Opposite: The sitting room has a particularly playful design, with the walls and chairs covered in cork. The orange sofa is a custom Nahem design, and sits atop a walnut platform table; the coffee table is by Percival Lafer.

In the den, the blackened steel and bright green lacquered wood bookcase, of Nahem's design, offers an unexpected source of bright color and a backdrop for his custom-designed sofa, club chairs, and rug. He continues using this pop of color in the bar area with a custom cabinet of his design. The steel and bright green lacquer create a contrast with the rich, organic texture of the whitewashed knotty pine walls.

Above: The new master bedroom was created from space that was once part of the double-height living room. Here, the dramatic pitch of the roof was rendered warmer by the ceiling with reclaimed barn wood. The upholstered headboard and walls, along with the nearly wall-to-wall rug and thick embroidered curtains, provide the space with abundant sound absorption and warmth.

Opposite: The master bathroom is an unexpected composition of Corian and teak. The slight nautical quality of these materials underscores the notion of this home as an escapist retreat.

Puck Penthouse

Located in lower Manhattan, this penthouse occupies the top two floors of a Romanesque Revival building that was built in the late 1800s for a prominent lithography company. Architect Jose Ramirez was responsible for the adaptive reuse and organization of much of the development's interior space. During the renovations, Ramirez added the second floor—which was essentially on the roof of the historic structure—and set this newly constructed space back from the facade to create usable outdoor spaces. The living and dining room, along with the kitchen, occupy the second floor, giving the rooms direct access to the terraces.

Following these significant changes, Nahem was commissioned to reorganize, furnish, and decorate the penthouse, and most importantly help mitigate the distinction between the newly constructed upper level and the century-old industrial lower level. Celebrating the existing texture and patina was the easy part; establishing that level of interest in the newly constructed areas, without falling into the trap of nostalgic mimicry, proved to be more of a challenge.

Nahem's clients, art collectors with a penchant for provocative contemporary art, were moving from a traditional uptown duplex and wanted something more casual that would still reflect their interest in collecting. Through the design, Nahem and his team successfully shifted interest from art to an impressive group of bespoke furnishings and handcrafted interior finishes.

While many of the rooms in the historic section of the penthouse feature dramatic barrel-vaulted ceilings and cast-iron columns, the newly constructed living and dining room and kitchen were devoid of such character. To resolve this problem, Nahem commissioned Amuneal, known for their custom metal work, to cover the ceiling with wood that had been sprayed with a metallic finish. Nahem continued to incorporate the custom work of artisans by installing a metal and glass chandelier by Christophe Côme, covering the walls in horsehair from John Boyd, collaborating with Ramirez, and designing a simple nickel fireplace with blackened bronze details. On the clients' suggestion, a tiled, vaulted ceiling replaced the Sheetrock one in the kitchen.

The room also features a dining table, a custom Nahem design of polished mirror-finish stainless and wood, which is the only rectilinear piece of furniture in the lofty living and dining room. While there are some vintage pieces in the home, Nahem's focus was to incorporate furnishings by various artisans he admired, like the settee in the living room by Chantal Saccomanno and Olivier Dayot. Nahem believes that the vintage craze of the last few decades has opened the door to craft-based one-of-a-kind furnishings. Here those pieces take on the stature and status once held by artworks within this style of contemporary interior.

The lower level houses the master bedroom, and features the more historic elements of the building, like barrel-vaulted ceilings. For this room and its outside hallway, Nahem installed a handcrafted soft mohair rug that runs up the lower half of the wall. He then had the artisans, who are from Guatemala, create a wall covering with the same yarn for the upper part of the wall. The two textiles are separated by a bronze cap. The end result is an all-encompassing texture-rich environment that is beautifully subtle, and also serves to buffer sound.

The more traditional approach to showcasing the historic patina of this penthouse would have been to create contrast with smooth white surfaces. Nahem, however, chose to move in the opposite direction: Texture and exquisite surfaces become an "all-over" backdrop for a spectacular collection of handcrafted furniture and art.

The entry provides testimony to the space's industrial past by introducing the rich plaster walls and barrel-vaulted brick ceilings that exist in many other parts of the home. The ottoman is a custom Nahem design in shaved mink with bronze legs, while the rug is a custom design supplied by Cristina Grajales in woven leather, gold-plated silver, and aluminum. Artwork by Christian Marclay hangs on the wall.

The ever-present grid of windows in the newly constructed living and dining room informed Nahem's design decisions in the space. He preferred the juxtaposition with organic shapes, which he incorporated in both the furnishings and the rug. Nahem designed the rug, which was made by Martin Patrick Evan, with a seemingly random serpentine edge, relying on the curvilinear contrast with the rigid geometry of the fenestration. Nahem designed the fire breast as a point of contrast to both the rug and the warm, natural materials present in the furnishings.

Following spread: Nahem worked with the fabricator Amuneal to create the custom ceiling treatment. Reclaimed wood was treated with a metallic finish to create the warm, reflective glow. As this room is part of the new construction, Nahem wanted the ceiling to be as much a statement as the barrel-vaulted brick evident in other parts of the home. A serpentine sofa, the de Sede DS-600, is covered in suede and leather. The room also includes a pair of club chairs by Jean Royère, a coffee table and rocker by Wendell Castle, which is covered in a vintage Afghan rug from the 1920s, and a settee by the artisans Chantal Saccomanno and Olivier Dayot.

The dining table is a custom Nahem design and was fabricated by Amuneal. The chairs are vintage French by Jules Leleu, circa 1955, and the chandelier and metal-and-glass credenza were designed by Christophe Côme. The space also features artwork by Chris Succo and Roy Lichtenstein.

The den, located right off the living and dining space, hosts a custom Nahem-designed bar and sofa. The walls are a combination of charred wood paneling by J Liston and mohair upholstery by Sacco Carpet. The pop-up coffee table is by Resource Furniture.

On the terrace, Nahem installed furniture by JANUS et Cie and Kenneth Cobonpue, and added a stainless spa by Diamond Spas.

Nahem created a barrel-vaulted ceiling in the kitchen to match the existing ceilings in the original part of the apartment. The pendant lights are by Angelo Lelli, and the kitchen stools are by Holly Hunt and covered in Toyine Sellers woven leather.

In the master bedroom suite, Nahem uses the walls and floor to create a stark contrast to the original barrel-vaulted ceiling. A blackened steel wall-hung cabinet with bookshelves, a custom Nahem design, hangs opposite the bed. The pair of chairs from the 1960s provides a place to sit while keeping the space visually open.

Here, a textile and rug were woven from the same mohair by artisans in Guatemala. The rug was then installed on the floor and the lower portion of the wall. The bed, which is a custom Nahem design, also incorporates the mohair. The effect is that of a luxurious cocoon. A hanging pod chair from Blackman Cruz occupies the far corner, and artwork by Adam McEwen hangs on the wall.

Second Home

Nahem's clients found this newly constructed home, which was built on spec, and purchased it because they loved the location and traditional feel. However, like nearly all homes built with the hope of finding a buyer, the developer was trying to appeal to the widest audience possible. Nahem's clients, already living in a home he had designed for them in the city, had grown accustomed to living in a bespoke environment. They were used to being in a space where every detail had been considered not only for its beauty and functionality, but also for how it met their specific needs and interests; this home needed some work.

Because it was their second home, the owners were open to something different from what Nahem had designed for them in the city. With that in mind, Nahem set about divorcing the structure from its intentionally generic inception. He understood that the traditional appeal of the home was in line with his clients' vision of downtime away from urban chaos, but also recognized that the awkward floor plan could be improved upon. Nahem had no interest in adhering to a specific historical moment or period; instead, he used the notion of the "traditional" as a vehicle to create a cozy home that he hoped would both foster relaxation and offer a delightful alternative to their more serious place in the city.

Steve Chrostowski of Alveary Architecture worked with Nahem on altering the home's spaces and increasing its size. Square footage was added to the living room, located on the ground floor, and to the master suite on the second. The architectural intervention also incorporated a separate sunroom into the living room, transforming it into a rectangular, sun-filled space that became the core of the home.

Nahem seized the opportunity provided by the traditional layout, with its singular, clearly defined rooms, to create a series of distinct spaces, all with strong identities—something modern environments with rooms that flow into each other often do not allow. Whimsical wallpapers, reclaimed wood, and colorful antique tiles were playfully used to create a sense of history and obliterate the feeling of "newness" that permeated the home. But because the newly created living room was open to the rest of the house, Nahem decided that simple white paint would be the logical choice for this space, and he eventually added coffers to the ceiling and a bay window. When the living room was finished, with furnishings from a range of periods sitting alongside potted palms, it was more reminiscent of the public spaces of a much-loved, long-established European seaside hotel than a suburban spec home.

The kitchen also follows in this theatrical vein, and is quite dramatic. Nahem coated the kitchen island with oxblood lacquer, covered the ceiling with dark reclaimed barn wood, and installed vibrant antique Portuguese tiles on the backsplash. In the adjacent dining room, Nahem added wallpaper and coral curtains, and in the first-floor den, which is smaller and more intimately scaled than the rest of the house, horizontal lengths of limed pecky cypress cover the walls.

The drama and infusion of character into the nondescript spaces continues in the master suite. While the bedroom has a neutral palette, the bathroom incorporates sea-green tiles on the walls and boldly geometric eighteenth-century Italian tiles on the floors. And because no opportunity to add character was lost, Nahem lined the tray ceiling here with whitewashed planks of reclaimed wood. By providing his clients with a colorful, textured, and varied environment for this second home, his design works to help them relax and decompress as it furthers the distance from their life—and their refined, yet monochromatic, home—in the city.

The living room is the center of this home, and an eclectic mix of furnishings and patterns gives the space a lived-in casual feeling. Nahem installed an antique French Empire limestone mantel, with a mirror attributed to the sculptor Paul Plumet directly above. A coffee table by Phillip Lloyd Powell sits in front of the fireplace. In the corner, Nahem added an antique Gustavian Swedish glass cabinet between paintings by Sarah McEneaney.

Nahem renders the room more intimate by creating two seating areas, one facing the fireplace and the other facing the entrance. A massive 1860s rag rug from Doris Leslie Blau with a bold pattern fills the room and provides an anchor for the multitude of forms, colors, and patterns used here. The sofas are a custom Nahem design, and one seating area includes a coffee table by René Prou and upholstered sculptural Swedish chairs by Kerstin Hörlin-Holmquist. A Wendell Castle table sits in front of the bay window.

The dining room incorporates wallpaper on the upper half of the wall with painted paneling in a dark olive on the lower half. The same dark olive paint is used on the ceiling. A pair of curtains with sheer linen over coral taffeta adds a sense of the unexpected and brightens the space, as does a sculptural dining table. Surrounding the table is a set of ash-framed upholstered Swedish dining chairs, circa 1940. A chandelier by Elis Bergh, circa 1920, hangs directly above. In the nook, Nahem placed a server by Charles Dudouyt below a rare Line Vautrin mirror.

In the breakfast area, the diversity of materials and styles becomes apparent. Here, a limestone floor is paired with a reclaimed fireplace mantel; a set of Danish modern dining chairs surrounds a circular table with a decidedly rustic feel. The kitchen ceiling is covered in reclaimed barn wood, which adds a dramatic feel. Tiles in a solid green-brown surround the intricately designed antique Portuguese tiles incorporated into the backsplash. This combination furthers the sense of all-over pattern, texture, and color that provides this space with a dramatic element.

Above: Nahem installed horizontal lengths of limed cypress in the den, where he hoped to take advantage of the room's smaller scale to create a more intimate space. The stone fireplace mantel, antique Louis XVI limestone with carved frieze, also offers a moment of contrast to the room's wood paneling. A bold chair by Finn Juhl pops against the room's neutral palette.

Opposite: Nahem added vintage wallpaper to one of the children's rooms, along with a rocking chair by Paul Laszlo and a French Arts and Crafts bookcase.

Because the master bedroom was intentionally left very neutral, the master bathroom was an opportunity to add some character. Nahem incorporated eighteenth-century Italian floor tiles with a whitewashed reclaimed barn wood ceiling, and added a Beaumont bathtub by Waterworks.

Gramercy Park Penthouse

When Nahem first saw this intimately scaled two-bedroom penthouse, it was a confusing warren with tiny windows. This didn't bother Nahem's client, though. He was drawn to its wraparound terraces and the potential of light-filled rooms, and was willing to sacrifice interior space for the potentially magnificent terrace.

The penthouse's sixteenth-floor location—it was essentially a structure built on the roof of a prewar building overlooking Gramercy Park—worked in Nahem's favor. With no one located above and windows that could not be seen from the street, making it exempt from the regulations of New York City's Landmarks Preservation Commission, he could freely reconfigure the space. As a consequence the layout was completely transformed to better meet the client's needs and to take advantage of the penthouse's connection to the outdoor space, which is now enjoyed from every room.

Nahem's client was familiar with his work. He had previously lived in a summer rental that Nahem had designed, and while he was not necessarily interested in decoration, he knew that Nahem understood how people lived and how to create inviting, well-functioning, comfortable spaces. With this in mind, Nahem set out to create an environment rich in texture and color, while still remaining neutral enough to host and showcase an ever-changing collection of contemporary art.

The core of the apartment is the connected living and dining room. In this space, Nahem divided the two functions with a fireplace that opens on both the living and dining sides. Nahem designed the firebox, a composition of hammered blackened steel and black Corian, to create a sharp contrast with the diamond coat plaster walls, which, like the ceilings, were left white. Perhaps the most notable feature in the living room is the partition of walnut and bronze mesh screens that runs along one wall. The screens provide the room with a great deal of color and texture, as well as much-needed storage. On the opposite wall, Nahem incorporated the same walnut and bronze mesh on cabinetry that surrounds the windows.

The screens, cabinetry, and neutral palette provide the main room with a notably architectural and masculine feel. It was also of utmost importance that everything be both comfortable and functional, because of the limited number of rooms in the home. Nahem installed a custom sofa, Nakashima cocktail table, and vintage Scandinavian wing chair atop a thick, woven rug. The window treatments were not chosen for privacy, but for their added texture and light control. While wall space for the client's art collection was limited due to Nahem's design alterations, they helped focus more attention on the few pieces that could be displayed at any one time.

For the kitchen, Nahem used polished, mirror-finish steel and glass for one of the upper cabinets in front of the windows. These materials reflect the view and allow for transparency. Nahem also continued to incorporate the walnut detail in both the cabinets and countertops, giving them a furniture-like feel and further integrating them with the rest of the apartment.

In the master bedroom, natural-tone fabric is used on the walls to add texture and warmth. As in the other rooms, color comes from the natural state of the various materials in the space: bronze, walnut, plaster, blackened steel, and travertine. For this project, Nahem moved away from color in favor of having a play on texture and materials, an approach he felt would provide his client with a highly functioning, neutral yet rich environment to showcase whatever artworks he was interested in at the moment.

Nahem and his client wanted to distinguish the entry from the living and dining room due to the small living quarters. In addition to being able to screen it off, Nahem wanted the space to have its own identity. Here, the diamond plaster was colored and travertine was chosen for the floor, which flows into the powder room.

In the living area, the fumed oak floors host a highly textured carpet upon which Nahem has gathered the furnishings, including a custom sofa of his own design, a George Nakashima cocktail table, a Scandinavian wing chair, and a pair of mid-century Pierre Paulin tulip lounge chairs. The fireplace, which opens on both the living room and dining area sides, was repositioned, a feat only possible because this space occupies the top floor of the building. The firebox was designed in hammered blackened steel and black Corian, and is a custom design by Nahem.

Following spread: The neutral Primovito rug, designed by Rosemary Hallgarten from ALT, contrasts with the bold colors of the Fred Tomaselli painting that hangs on the far wall.

The walnut and bronze mesh screens conceal both storage and a bar, and can also be used to render the living and dining room private from the entry. For this room, Nahem chose old-growth fumed oak for the floors, which he saw as a nod to the prewar history of the residential building.

To ground the lower cabinets in the kitchen, Nahem added a walnut detail he calls crenellation—a technique in which walnut panels are channeled in a striated pattern—to both the sides and the drawer fronts. The kitchen opens out to the terrace, which includes a dining banquette by Alec Gunn.

In the master bedroom, most of the color comes from the materials: bronze, walnut, and fabrics composed of natural materials. The walls shift from white diamond coat plaster to upholstered walls in a natural, neutral fabric, which creates a more intimate space and buffers noise. The bed, which is of Nahem's own design, is a composition of walnut, fabric, and leather and includes a headboard that incorporates a pair of side tables.

Central Park West Landmark

Perhaps one of New York's most prestigious addresses, this apartment is located in a neo-Renaissance English Victorian building from the 1880s. In addition to being a New York City Landmark, it is also on the National Register of Historic Places and a National Historic Landmark. In order to maintain this status, the Upper West Side building does not permit any alterations to the original configuration of the spaces; so while Nahem was able to make minor adjustments, dealing with the historic space mandated that the majority of the walls remain in place.

The six-room apartment, organized around the French idea of *enfilade* (which was associated with the notion of refined living at the time the building was constructed), provided Nahem with a traditional layout of connected living spaces and set much of the tone for how the rooms would be appointed and furnished. Nahem's client was drawn to the gravitas of the space, with its original details and twelve-foot ceilings, and hoped for a traditional environment that would celebrate the history of the location. Nahem brought these ideas into focus. While he respected the client's mandate of traditional furnishings and finishes, Nahem's eclectic background encouraged him to mix things up.

In order to call attention to the above-average ceiling heights throughout, Nahem installed large, impactful chandeliers wherever possible. The original wood trim, which was an omnipresent sea of library brown, too serious and heavy for the lifestyle Nahem envisioned for his client, was stripped, raked, and limed. The change exalts the original millwork, but also renders it more furniture-like and provides an unexpected contemporary feeling throughout the apartment. The limed woodwork, along with the dusty palette and eclectic furnishings Nahem incorporated, shifts the character of the apartment from the late Victorian interiors of a public academic space like a library or museum to a lavish and intimate contemporary home with a strong dose of the theatrical.

Because the apartment was once part of the public space of the building, specifically a series of dining rooms for residents, it lacked a proper sense of entry. Nahem mitigated this by moving the living room walls that flanked the fireplace to allow for more room in the foyer. The entry, with its rich walls and spot lighting, introduces the theatricality of the spaces that lie beyond and prepares visitors for the dramatic and unexpected.

Throughout the home Nahem incorporates many sinuous furnishings from the middle of the twentieth century that were, at the time, "traditional." Today, however, these pieces occupy an interesting place as they harken back to two distinct periods—while they are clearly of their time, they were intended then to call to mind a different time. The dining room, for example, combines "traditional" dining chairs designed by Nahem with a distinctively 1950s feel, bold traditional textiles used as curtains, and a 1970s parchment table. Nahem also folds into this mix unexpected color and pattern. The lilac-and-black hand-embroidered wall covering used in the master bedroom, for example, recalls some of the dusty hues used in other rooms, but it certainly provides a moment of surprise and delight. Throughout the apartment, Nahem has created a layered sense of the traditional that refuses to be static and therefore feels very luxurious and contemporary.

The entry foyer offers a glimpse of the theatricality present throughout the entire apartment. Nahem installed a French Empire table, circa 1815, with a mirror by Eve Kaplan hanging directly above.

Dramatic lighting fixtures are used throughout the home to take full advantage of the ceiling heights, which are more than twelve feet high. Here, in the living room, the chandelier is by Napoleon Martinez for Venini. The sitting area includes a sofa by Muriel Brandolini, a coffee table by Ramsey, and American chairs, circa 1940.

While the client's mandate was traditional, Nahem's eclectic background encouraged him to mix things up. Hanging above the antique fireplace, with its nineteenth-century Louis XVI marble mantel, is a rare George I Giltwood mirror, circa 1725, from Hyde Park Antiques. Beneath the mix of furnishings in the room is a vintage Oushak Borle rug.

The intimately scaled dining room combines traditional dining chairs in dusty purple mohair velvet with embroidered detail on the back with a 1970s-era parchment table. The room also includes a Swedish birch Caesar cabinet by Axel Einar Hjorth, circa 1930, from H.M. Luther, and a hand-embroidered wall covering from Fromental. Throughout the apartment, the wood trim, original to the building's construction, was stripped, raked, and limed. The gesture helps divorce the space from the 1880s while still celebrating its magnificent details, thus opening the door to a wide spectrum of periods.

In the more casual sitting room, an "L" shaped sofa is paired with a vintage Ward Bennett chair and Tommi Parzinger coffee table. The paintings depicting Venice above the sofa were commissioned from the artist Roger de Montebello.

In the master bedroom, Nahem continues to play with periods. Here, the hand-embroidered fabric used to upholster the walls seamlessly spills onto the headboard, where the pattern meticulously lines up with that on the wall. A variation of the fabric is also used on the windows. The unexpected hue is simultaneously whimsical and stately. The vanity table, designed by Nahem, ingeniously conceals a television and speakers. The surface transforms into a simple mirror when the television is not in use.

The master bedroom suite contains a bathroom and dressing room of current proportions. These spaces were created from what was once an adjacent bedroom. In the ample dressing room, Nahem extends his use of raked and limed woodwork to the cabinetry.

Neo-Grec Townhouse

When Nahem's clients purchased this stately Neo-Grec townhouse on Manhattan's notoriously elegant Upper East Side the only thing regal about it was its decaying limestone facade. The majestic construction had been divided up into a warren of apartments; nearly all of its century-plus of architectural details had been either removed or destroyed. Time and wear had taken their toll. The five-story structure required a gut renovation, and the architect Jose Ramirez of J. L. Ramirez Architects, along with Joe Nahem, was charged with the task of transforming the makeshift apartment building into a gracious and highly functioning home for a young couple and their small children.

Because the building sits in a historic district, New York City's Landmarks Preservation Commission required that the street-facing facade remain as it was originally constructed. As a consequence, the placement and height of the windows had to remain as they were. With this constraint, it made sense to restore the room functions and organization to something resembling the building's original plan as a single-family home. Ramirez worked closely with Fox-Nahem, with whom he had collaborated before on other projects, to return the home to its original splendor, organization, and character while infusing it with the necessities of modern life: A large kitchen was returned to the garden level and dining and formal living rooms were installed above, with family space and bedrooms above that. An elevator and stairwell were also added, along with powder rooms, contemporary-scaled bathrooms, and closets.

The house was essentially rebuilt from the ground up, providing Nahem with an opportunity to not only furnish but also direct the construction of each room's envelope. The property's location, coupled with its grand facade, historic pedigree, and traditional layout might have directed the designer toward formal solutions for the interior. However, Nahem, taking cues from his clients, embarked in a different direction, using design elements like wall coverings, ceiling treatments, textiles, flooring, furnishings, and art, to create a sense of grandeur. The interior is grounded not in notions of preciousness, but rather in creative value.

Nahem sought to infuse the interiors with a sense of surprise and discovery wherever possible. Unexpected and highly crafted materials, patterns, and finishes are used with abandon. While these elements certainly align with the youthful tastes of the occupants, they also move beyond any identifiable contemporary trend and into the rarefied space traditionally reserved for a style that becomes an architectural legacy. The sinuous staircase, for example, is a prominent feature of the home; it runs up all flights, and occupants are never more than one room away from it. Nahem designed a stair rail in bronze and transparent glass rods. The material both elevates the bronze and adds a sense of reflected light into the windowless core of the building. This type of surprising detail is incorporated throughout the home, often in unforeseen spots. Nahem commissioned the artist Matthew Solomon of Maison Gerard, known for his porcelain floral arrangements, to develop a tracery for the dining room ceiling. The resulting installation calls to mind the ornate plaster decorations once found in Upper East Side mansions, but is decidedly modern in its embrace of the organic. In essence, Nahem has created interiors that seem to have the innate capacity of self-preservation—details and surfaces of such rigor, one could hardly fathom their removal.

The entry vestibule features back-painted glass, which was commissioned by Fox-Nahem and fabricated in New York by Sublime Living. In addition to its durability, Nahem chose this material because he hoped it would create depth, reflectivity, and visual interest in an otherwise dark entry space. The entry also includes lighting by Paavo Tynell and a mirror by Michele Ghiro.

Because the staircase is ever-present, Nahem designed the handrail in bronze, and alternated the balusters in bronze and glass to add transparency and a reflective quality in the windowless core of the home. The walls feature molding-frame panels of hand-painted silk from Fromental, and a pair of Carlo Bugatti chairs flank a wall-hung cabinet by James Bearden. Artwork by Rudolf Stingel is positioned directly above, and an ottoman designed by Nahem and David Gorman also occupies the hallway.

Above: In the breakfast room off the kitchen, the walls are covered with mirror and trellised wood, which was painted white. The one-of-a-kind table is by Jorge Pardo and is framed by a custom Fox-Nahem-designed banquette in orange leather. Glazed stoneware by Ka-Kwong Hui, circa 1967, sits in the windowsill.

Right: The kitchen cabinets have a painted stria finish and bronze trim, and are a Fox-Nahem custom design for St. Charles. The walls also feature the same stria finish. A pair of bold fixtures from Apparatus hangs from the hand-troweled plaster ceiling. To complete the room, Nahem added tiles from Ann Sacks to the floor.

Above: Nahem installed a Hechizoo custom runner from Cristina Grajales in the hallway between the dining and living rooms. He also added a Carlo Bugatti hanging shelf and a light fixture by David Wiseman.

Right: In the dining room, Fox-Nahem commissioned the artist Matthew Solomon to create the ceiling porcelain detail, inspired by the classic plaster tracery found in similar townhouses. The walls are a combination of wood paneling with sound-absorbing brocade fabric. The dining tables and chairs are custom Fox-Nahem designs, and were created with versatility in mind; they can be used separately or transform into one large table that can accommodate sixteen.

Opposite: In the living room, diamond coat plaster walls and plaster-framed inset panels are paired with an antique marble mantelpiece, which Nahem found in England, and 1930s sconces by Seguso Vetri d'Arte. The one-of-a-kind cabinet beside the fireplace is a contemporary piece by the artist Roland Mellan. It is composed of a series of brass plates in to which a variety of colored enamels are poured, much like cloisonné. Nahem also added to the room a chair by Jorge Zalszupin and wall lamps by Felix Agostini.

Following spread: A silk rug, designed in collaboration with Sacco Carpet, functions as an elegant and timeless background for the eclectic furnishings and finishes in the space. The sofa is a custom Fox-Nahem design, and on either side are side tables by Osanna Visconti di Modrone. Two chairs by Gio Ponti surround the gilded Wendell Castle coffee table. The room also includes artwork by Ryan McGinness and Chris Martin.

A custom Fox-Nahem-designed L-shaped sofa in handwoven mohair fabric and leather creates a welcoming spot in the paneled den, and is paired with a commissioned coffee table by Mattia Bonetti and artwork by Pentti Monkkonen. Here, the walls were covered with worn, whitewashed pine and hand-stitched suede. The bar, also designed by Nahem, is fabricated in clear and oxidized copper and creates a destination at the back of the room. It sits beside a vintage Osvaldo Borsani game table, circa 1955, with chairs by Louis Sognot.

The goal for the master bedroom was to create a tranquil, quiet, and luxurious retreat. While the room maintains a light, neutral palette, the glossy gray ceiling provides depth and visual interest. The bed, a custom Fox-Nahem design, displays a sense of movement and whimsy; it was fabricated from turned walnut, and includes gilded spheres in the head and footboards. The bedside "UFO" tables, in black-stained oak and bronze, are by Mattia Bonetti, and were custom sized for this project. To the right of the fireplace sits a vintage Josef Frank "Flora" cabinet, circa 1937.

The master bath is a study in Carrara and silver tones. Here, marble tile, Bianco Carrara Lotus from Artistic Tile, lines the walls and adds texture. The Candide tub with fittings from the Opus Collection, both from Waterworks, provides contrast in form and hue. The fixture above the tub is by Thaddeus Wolfe and the vanity is a custom design by Nahem.

Chelsea Penthouse

Joe Nahem worked on this penthouse apartment, which occupies the eleventh and twelfth floors of a newly constructed apartment building, when his client, the building's developer, was in the midst of construction, and again some thirteen years later after his client's family had grown. When Nahem first visited the construction site, he noticed the view of the gilded dome of the neighboring building, which was erected in the late nineteenth century as a department store and had since been converted into housing. Nahem noted that it was unfortunate that the impressive view would be lost behind the solid brick exterior wall. Within days his client called to say that the solid wall on the east-facing side of the living room could be replaced by glass, and Nahem and his late partner Tom Fox worked with the construction team to install an impressive grid of nearly ceiling-to-floor windows in its place.

Revealing the architectural detail of the nearby building and bringing the dome's warm reflection into the space inspired Nahem to imbue the apartment's interiors with rich reflective and often metallic surfaces of their own. Some twelve varieties, colors, and finishes of Venetian plaster were used in the public spaces, even on the ceilings. In order to mitigate the "Sheetrock-box" quality of the new construction, Nahem incorporated materials with a certain depth wherever possible. The plaster was clearly chosen for its gravity and variation within a monochromatic world of neutral and metallic tones, as were the reclaimed, antique Grey Barr limestone floors. The result creates a depth of color throughout the apartment while not incorporating any specific hue.

At first glance, the furnishings in this relatively sparse space seem quite disparate, as if any notion of an overriding style or approach had been abandoned in favor of a free association of great objects that simply look good together. In much the same way that no one color dominates the space, no specific style of furniture sets a single tone; instead, they all work together to create a comfortable and livable environment. In the living room, for example, Nahem combines a custom bar of his own design in bronze and leather, a pair of Modern French armchairs from the 1940s, a decidedly handcrafted George Nakashima chaise, a pair of Danish Modern chairs by Ib Kofod-Larsen, and a custom Nahem-designed sofa with a traditional feel. But Nahem explains that his idea was to bring beautiful yet simple things together that would serve their purposes: "When a home has various rooms, how do you get people to use the space? You do that by collecting beautiful things that work together." His masterful mixing of styles, along with the nearly monochromatic palette, provides the space with a notably timeless quality. However, this did not prevent Nahem from experimenting when the opportunity presented itself. For rooms more isolated from the other spaces—like the den and master bedroom—Nahem felt freer to incorporate color and more complex fabrics. Throughout this home, Nahem establishes a contrast between the subtle and the overt. We see this shift from room to room, but also within individual spaces. The subtle complexity of the Venetian plaster exists in stark contrast to the dramatic antique firebox in the living room, for example, and this contrast seems to refer back to the contrast between the newly constructed building and the gleaming gilded dome in the distance.

Above: For the dining area wall, which is located opposite the firebox and the gilded view in the living room, Nahem incorporated bronze and silver-leaf powder into the plaster. This technique is responsible for both the color and the organic quality, and was done by Nota Design. The rosewood and brass server is by Jean Royère, circa 1937, and is paired with a Line Vautrin mirror.

Left: In the dining room, the dining chairs—which are 1950s vintage in gilded iron by André Arbus—were upholstered in leather with Lurex and then trimmed in black horsehair. The table, a custom design by Nahem, was sprayed with an automotive-grade high-gloss silver lacquer, the same paint used on Mercedes-Benz cars.

After working closely with Alveary Architecture and the construction team to install the floor-to-ceiling window, Nahem added a vintage firebox in front of the window and finished it with an eighteenth-century French Louis XVI stone fireplace surround. Sitting in front is a rare circa-mid-1950s George Nakashima lounge chair fabricated from black walnut with a webbed seat and back, alongside a chair by Ib Kofod-Larsen.

Above: Furnishings from JANUS et Cie were used on the terrace. The gilded dome of the neighboring building can be seen in the distance.

Right: In the living room, the custom Nahem-designed sofa distinguishes the dining area from the living room, and is paired with a set of 1940s French chairs with swooping backs that are in stark contrast to the pair of lb Kofod-Larsen chairs in a decidedly late-1950s Danish style. Artwork by Chris Martin is also featured prominently. The furnishings here are seemingly disparate stylistically; Nahem's goal was to simply put pieces together that looked nice and would serve their purpose, leaving the space free of any overriding concept. The result strikes a unique balance between elegant and casual.

Left: The bar, which is a custom Nahem design and made by PLANT, is constructed in bronze and leather. Its shape was inspired by the room and it is fully functional with both a sink and an ice maker.

Following spread: The den features an eclectic mix of colors and textures, with a mid-century Scandinavian Märta Måås-Fjetterström rug acting as the backdrop. The sofa, a custom Nahem design, is made with handwoven fabric by Toyine Sellers, and is paired with a vintage Brazilian rosewood table.

In lieu of wainscoting in the breakfast room, Nahem used an upholstered panel to soften the space. The banquette, by Osvaldo Borsani, was upholstered in woven leather and paired with a custom-designed Corian table with a wooden insert. Hanging above is a photograph by Adam Fuss. The chairs are vintage and were designed by Pierre Guariche. The kitchen cabinets are a high-gloss lacquer and the counters are Corian paired with a stainless
steel backsplash.

In the master bedroom, Nahem abandons the Venetian plaster and instead upholsters the walls in a rich blue woven fabric, distinguishing this room from the rest of the house and rendering it both more personal and more intimate. Nahem also added raked and limed trim and furnishings, including the custom Nahem-designed bed, which incorporates an upholstered headboard in contrasting beige, and a pair of highly decorated chests of drawers by Josef Frank. Sitting atop the chest of drawers are Murano glass lamps, circa 1950s, by Gio Ponti; lamps by Georges Pelletier sit on the bedside tables; and paintings by Erik Benson hang above the bed.

The walls in the master bath were covered in book-matched slabs of an unexpected Brazilian stone. The blue stone carries the chromatic theme introduced in the bedroom. The vanity is a custom Nahem design made of polished steel and cement.

Connecticut Reinterpreted

Nahem's clients purchased this 1920s-era Colonial Revival Connecticut property in the late 1990s, and hired Mica Ertegun to decorate the interiors in the home's traditional vein. But as their art collection grew to include the likes of John Baldessari, Richard Prince, Damien Hirst, Jeff Koons, Gerhard Richter, and Cindy Sherman, they longed for a more minimal space with abundant white walls.

While Nahem was happy to remove some of the moldings, which had made hanging large artworks an awkward endeavor, he did not want to create an interior that would disregard the traditional exterior and floor plan. In keeping with his clients' desire, he left most of the walls white or a variation of pale gray, with the exception of the dining room and bar. When it came to furnishing the space, Nahem encouraged his clients to use some of the same criteria that they had so astutely applied when building their art collection with their choice of furnishings. The end result is a showplace for provocative art and bold contemporary furnishings that challenges traditional ideas of formality.

Throughout the interiors, Nahem plays with notions of surprise and discovery, and attempts, wherever possible, to foster a dialogue between the furnishings and decorative choices and the artworks. In the living room, for example, artworks by Jeff Koons, Andy Warhol, and Gerhard Richter share the space with a highly reflective metal settee by Ron Arad, a collection of mid-century club chairs in a brilliant pale turquoise velvet by Gio Ponti, and a curvilinear sofa of Nahem's own design, which sits in an almost calligraphic swirl of hand-forged bronze rod.

Juxtapositions of art, furnishings, function, and comfort are used to create tension and interest throughout the home and these combinations often elevate both the art and the interior design. In the hallway, for example, a large polished stainless steel cabinet by Damien Hirst, which contains a vast number of actual English pills, ironically leads the way to the bar. In the dining room, Nahem continues to create relationships that foster interest not only in the individual pieces of art but in the furnishings and decorative choices as well. The centerpiece of this room is a massive chandelier, on which Nahem collaborated with David Wiseman through R & Company, who is known for his work with porcelain and bronze. This piece appears to be growing out of the ceiling, with bronze "branches" descending to porcelain blossoms that host lights. Beneath the chandelier sits a circular table, designed by Nahem, in powder-coated steel. The room's dark green lacquered walls enhance the white table and porcelain blossoms, but the color also brings to mind the promise of growth and breathes life into Wiseman's whimsical chandelier.

Even though his clients' interest in and appreciation of provocative contemporary art made them long for a blank white container for their collection, Nahem encouraged them to reconsider the role the decorative arts might have in their home. The end result is an inviting interior that plays by the rules established by this traditional colonial home while simultaneously defying all expectations.

Above: The living room contains an eclectic mix of furniture and artwork by Jeff Koons, Andy Warhol, and Gerhard Richter. Perhaps as a nod to the home's traditional architecture and organization, Nahem sits this highly unexpected composition of furnishings—like the turquoise armchairs, upholstered in gleaming velvet, by Gio Ponti, and the white Pierre Paulin chair—atop a massive nineteenth-century Amritsar rug in its traditional golden hues.

Opposite and following page: Continuing with the theme of surprise and discovery, Nahem pairs two eighteenth-century Swedish consoles in the manner of Louis Jean Desprez with more modern sculptures, like this piece by Jeff Koons.

Nahem divided the room into two distinct seating areas: One, in front of the fireplace, hosts a Nahem-designed kidney-shaped sofa with a very distinctive forged-bronze base of swirling curves. The other, in the bay window, revolves around a metal settee by Ron Arad.

Nahem chose a dark green lacquer for the dining room walls, which provides contrast for the Nahem-designed dining table and the David Wiseman porcelain-and-bronze chandelier. To install Nahem's table, the floor had to be removed, the table bolted to the structure of the home, and the floor replaced. As a result, the table appears to float within the space. Nahem also designed the dining chairs. The room hosts artwork by Mark Grotjahn, Richard Prince, and Mike Kelly.

In the library, which also serves as the TV room, Nahem added a cerused finish to the paneling and installed art by Sean Landers. The chairs, upholstered in a faux bois pattern, are custom Nahem designs and were created for comfort as well as visual interest. The sofa is also a custom Nahem design and sits between lamps by Roberto Giulio Rida. The fossilized stone top coffee table, from the mid-1980s, is by Michael Taylor.

The centerpiece of this intimately scaled room is the bar, of Nahem's own design, which incorporates a mirror panel that reveals a flat-screen TV with the flip of a switch. The walls have been covered in faux suede and feature a large Cindy Sherman photograph as well as a bright aluminum panel by the artist Rudolf Stingel. A mirrored pill cabinet by Damien Hirst can be seen in the hallway. The room also hosts a sofa by Vladimir Kagan, Giancarlo Piretti chairs, and a Giacometti coffee table.

The den and game room beyond are perhaps the most informal rooms in the house. Nahem embraces this idea of play with a custom sofa in two different woven fabrics. The rug and fireplace are also custom Nahem designs. The fireplace has a rectilinear design with a vertical band of cutouts; Tibetan textiles inspired the rug design, which, like the fireplace, incorporates a series of geometric cutouts. Nahem worked with the rug manufacturer to create the unique uneven edge.

Nahem transformed what was originally a screened-in porch into a game room. The room now hosts a giant Damien Hirst butterfly collage. Nahem also closed off one of the entryways to the room with a suspended set of shelves in mirror steel, which still provides visual access to the space.

The master bedroom suite originally incorporated a sitting room, which Nahem removed in order to provide the owners with more closet space and his-and-hers spa baths. On the far wall hangs a large abstract painting by Willem de Kooning. The swirling headboard, a custom Nahem design, is a composition of Corian and upholstery. The window-niche sofa is also a custom Nahem design, and matches the velvet-covered chair by Joaquim Tenreiro.

The design of the dressing room is the result of consultations with stylists and an inventory of the owners' wardrobe. The room's centerpiece is an elliptical dresser finished in silver metallic lacquer with glass display shelves suspended above.

For this ample master bathroom, Fox-Nahem lined the walls with a white architectural glass typically used on the facade of skyscrapers. The ingenious use of materials creates a reflective surface that brings in light and is virtually maintenance free. Here, the designers contrasted this ultra smooth material with custom metal and resin panels, which they had fabricated by Based Upon. The hanging pendant is by Vistosi.

A Stanford White Townhouse

When Nahem's clients purchased this storied Manhattan townhouse, it was being used as office space. While much of the facade had retained the original splendor of Stanford White's 1904 design, most of the interior of the imperially scaled, twenty-three-foot-wide, six-story structure had failed to maintain that grandeur.

Nahem was hired by his client to both design the building's interiors and direct the architectural intervention required to return the structure to its original function as a family home. When Nahem took the lead, he helped select architect Thomas Vail, and the team embarked on a total, eighteen-month-long, gut renovation and restoration, largely inspired by White's initial design. While most of the rooms remained where White had originally located them, some of the spaces, specifically the master bedroom, had to be altered to accommodate a contemporary master suite. The windows and all systems, along with crown moldings, plasterwork, and flooring, were replaced according to Nahem and Vail's design. The only parts of the original structure that the team was able to restore were the stairwell balustrade and dining room paneling.

While Nahem's clients embraced the history of their new home, they did not want to live in a hyper-formal Stanford White interior. Nor did they want the home to feel out of sync with their relaxed lifestyle and collection of contemporary art. However, White's original design established some very formal rooms, and Nahem felt that the vertical organization of the house—which demanded a certain amount of segregation between the rooms—supported a more formal approach. Nahem was able to mitigate this formality with his clients' desire for a more inviting environment with unexpected color, furnishings, art, and exuberant, often vintage fabrics.

Like most townhomes, the space was originally designed to go from public to private as it moved from the ground floor to the upper floors, and Nahem and his team maintained this organization. By 1904 single-family homes located in the Upper East Side were being built for the very wealthy and were much grander in scale than townhomes that populated downtown neighborhoods. Part of this newfound luxury meant architects omitted the stoop, allowing for a grander foyer and a more modern entry sequence. Nahem was not afraid to celebrate the power and scale of this space, and created an elegant limestone-paved foyer that also serves as a gallery.

In the living room, a moody blue-gray became the backdrop for the clients' ever-changing art collection. Nahem combines mid-century furnishings by the likes of Billy Haines with Baccarat lamps and European antiques, and this mash-up of styles and periods helps soften the formal quality of the space. The same play of new and old, expected and unexpected continues in the dramatic dining room. Nahem restored and re-stained the original oak walls, and installed an eighteenth-century Venetian glass chandelier; he then challenges that expected gesture with a photograph by Cindy Sherman hung over a signed 1948 sideboard by André Arbus.

Nahem set out to create an environment that matched the importance of the structure without conceding to the temptations to render the spaces excessively precious. Important furnishings and art were made more accessible through the use of exuberant textiles and fabrics, many from Cora Ginsburg. In addition, the design maintained a "family first" mantra. The top floor of the home, for example, had been designed by White as an art studio for its original owner, Charles Dana Gibson, famed creator of the Gibson Girls illustrations. Along with Vail, Nahem and his team ingeniously transformed the space into an indoor gymnasium complete with a basketball court with a regulation three-point line.

In the living room, Nahem placed a French cabinet by André Arbus, circa 1940s, and hung a Georgia O'Keeffe painting directly above. Sitting atop the cabinet is a tea set by Joseph Hoffman.

In the limestone-paved foyer, a playful oversized work on paper by Robert Rauschenberg underscores the grandeur of the space while undermining its formality. A magnificent reproduction swinging door with leaded glass and copper plating leads to the kitchen. Sitting nearby are chairs by Raymond Subes.

Right: The furniture and art are equally as eclectic in the living room, with tufted chairs by Billy Haines, a cocktail table by Diego Giacometti, and an Ed Ruscha painting.

Previous spread: Nahem chose a blue-gray color for the walls of the living room, which houses a collection of diverse objects from a wide range of periods. Nahem installed a nineteenth-century American marble fireplace mantel, with Ruhlmann sconces on either side, and above it he hung a Venetian mirror from the turn of the last century. He traveled further back in time, to the eighteenth century, for the Italian chandelier.

Above: The stair hall has original Stanford White railing with alternating balustrades, and features art by Willem de Kooning and Georgia O'Keeffe.

Opposite: The dining room is perhaps the most dramatic room in the house. In this space, Nahem continued to mix periods and styles in unexpected ways. In a nod to the serious historical pedigree of the home, he restored the oak paneling and hung an eighteenth-century Venetian glass chandelier above the massive custom Nahem-designed table. He then took a turn toward the contemporary, hanging an impressive photograph by Cindy Sherman over a sideboard by André Arbus from 1948.

The kitchen remained where it had originally been located, just off the ground-floor foyer. However, Nahem rendered the space more welcoming and family-friendly by adding a brown leather banquette for casual meals, along with a period wood-burning stove.

Above: The clients knew they wanted a space to serve the entire family, but what had been designed as a top-floor art studio for the home's original owner presented a challenge for Nahem, Vail, and his clients. Eventually transforming the space into a basketball court that could double as a playroom seemed like the perfect, albeit unexpected, solution.

Right: Nahem designed a custom sofa with cast bronze legs for the library, and added a George Nakashima table to the space.

The area of the home that required the most reconfiguration was the master suite. Rooms were shifted to create space for closets, a master bath, and an ample master bedroom. The fireplace in the room, which could not be moved, was off center once the reconfiguration was complete, and Nahem compensated for this with an oversized headboard of his own design. Nahem also added photographs by Man Ray above the bed.

Nahem and Vail added the round window in the master bathroom. They thought this would be in keeping with the Stanford White architecture and, luckily, Landmarks approved the addition.

Architecture and Design

Nahem's clients had lived in a 1960s-era modernist home on this site before hiring the architect Annabelle Selldorf to provide guidance in updating and enlarging the space. Selldorf initially explored building an extension and increasing the indoor-outdoor flow, but after much consideration, both Selldorf and the owners realized that new, ground-up construction was in order.

Selldorf's experience as a designer of both private homes and public exhibition spaces made her the perfect choice for these clients: gallery owners with galleries in New York and London and a substantial collection they hoped to eventually install here. While much of the renovation was a complete overhaul, the original home had a courtyard that was beloved by the owners. Selldorf duplicated that gesture with a new garden-like entry on one side of the property and eighty feet of sliding glass doors, which open to a terrace and pool, along the other.

Selldorf's mahogany-clad construction was in the midst of being finished when Nahem was called in to furnish this masterfully designed modernist home. Under Nahem's direction a layer of thoughtful decoration was added. Selldorf had organized the public rooms off the common corridor, which runs along the window wall and provides most of the ground floor with an open, continuous feeling. This meant that Nahem's use of color had to be very calculated. It could not disrupt Selldorf's rhythm of sequential rooms as seen from the common space, but it could be explored once inside those spaces on the walls opposite the windows. Specific walls moved away from white to embrace color and texture through the use of various paints and reclaimed barn wood. In the living room, for example, Nahem painted the far wall in a warm tan. He then continued with that color into the corridor and study beyond, where the walls shift to the reclaimed barn wood. A similar strategy was used in the dining room, which had access to windows in the hallway, but not within. Nahem painted the far wall with a highly reflective peacock-blue automotive paint. It added a specific character to the room, and helped brighten the space.

Nahem also set out to push the gallery-like, public space quality of the home in a notably domestic and personal direction. Selldorf had, for example, designed the home with recessed pockets in the ceiling for solar shades. Nahem took her lead, but then used those same pockets to conceal tracks for yards of sheer linen draperies. Nahem believed that having a shade that disappeared into a pocket might be practical, though it would leave the windows bare when the shades were up and cut off when closed. He also knew that walls of glass would turn to black, cold reflective surfaces at night, and neither be engaging nor foster a sense of intimacy and comfort within the space.

On many levels, this project reflects the conflicting goals of contemporary architecture and decoration. Nahem hoped to create a dynamic environment through the incorporation of color, texture, and variation—ideas that often contradict contemporary architecture's interest in consistency and maintaining a minimal palette of materials. Whether using reclaimed barn wood or lacquered Sheetrock, Nahem believed he could incorporate such devices without diminishing the goals of the architect, and certainly not diminishing the dramatic impact of his clients' art and furniture collection. Nahem understood that his clients, practiced connoisseurs of modernism, wanted to avoid anything decorative or superfluous; however, he also understood that they wanted a comfortable, inviting home, and pushed them to think beyond the notion of a home as a white box.

The entry introduces Annabelle Selldorf's modernist *enfilade* of public rooms, which share an eighty-foot length of sliding glass doors along the ocean side of the home. Nahem has installed a massive vintage Murano-glass pendant light, a hundred-pound collection of glittering glass rosettes, in the central three-story stairwell. The entry table, a rare Nanna Ditzel in lacquered fiberglass from 1969, sits atop a Berit Koenig Swedish rug from 1950. Artwork by Richard Prince hangs on the wall.

In this corner of the living room, Nahem pairs a Frits Henningsen high-back wing chair, which was designed in 1935, with a Traccia occasional table by Meret Oppenheim from 1972. The room also hosts a custom sofa of Nahem's own design atop a massive antique Oushak rug and a sculpture by Rebecca Warren.

Positioned below a Martin Kippenberger painting, a kidney-shaped Cloud sofa by Vladimir Kagan is paired with two Czechoslovakian lounge chairs by Jindrich Halabala, and surround a French coffee table, circa 1958, by Michel Mangematin. A painting by Georg Baselitz hangs above the fireplace and is next to a rare French cabinet, circa 1950s, by Jacques Adnet.

Previous spread: Color was used carefully and in limited ways so as to not interfere with the art collection, like the painting by Albert Oehlen. In the living room, for example, Nahem used a vibrant blue hide on a classic Mies van der Rohe bench, and then painted the far wall in a dark tan. Nahem was careful to designate entire architectural volumes with color as opposed to single walls, as seen in the color on the living room wall, which wraps around into the corridor and study beyond.

Nahem installed reclaimed barn wood in the study off the living room, an unexpected gesture for this modernist structure. In the corner, Nahem has provided a place to work. Through the window, there is a glimpse of the courtyard entry. Installed above the fireplace, the Cindy Sherman photograph, a self-portrait with an otherworldly presence, appears to preside over the room. The bookshelves flanking the fireplace were designed by Vittorio Introini in 1969.

Following spread: A painting by George Condo hangs above the sofa, which is a custom Nahem and David Gorman design. The "Clam" chair is by Philip Arctander, and the chandelier hanging above is by Gino Sarfatti.

Nahem painted the far wall of the dining room in a reflective peacock-blue automotive paint with the hope that the reflective quality of the wall would add light and a sense of brightness into the room. Nahem then hung his clients' Paul Evans console from 1969 on the wall. Artworks by George Condo and Cindy Sherman also make an impression in the dining room, alongside other unique pieces. The live edge table by woodworker Mira Nakashima is paired with chairs from The Future Perfect and sits atop a patchwork of hides by Martin Patrick Evan.

The tiled backsplash adds a pop of color to the kitchen. Both the Corian kitchen table and banquette are custom designs by Nahem. The island has pendant lighting from Studio Van den Akker hanging above, with vintage barstools for seating.

Following spread: The color palette shifts in the upstairs den to deep silver. The gray flannel sofa, with deep horizontal ribbing, is a custom Nahem design.

The centerpiece of the master bedroom is an upholstered bed, headboard, and bedside table, which is a custom Nahem design. A one-of-a-kind desk by George Nakashima from 1972 proudly occupies the far corner of the bedroom, and an artwork by George Condo hangs above built-in millwork by Selldorf Architects.

Storied Park Avenue Duplex

740 Park Avenue has a unique history; the building was constructed in 1929 by James T. Lee, Jacqueline Kennedy Onassis's grandfather, and designed by the famed architects Rosario Candela and Arthur Loomis Harmon. But Nahem's clients dove further into this storied pedigree by actually purchasing the duplex apartment that Jacqueline Kennedy Onassis (née Bouvier) grew up in. Needless to say, the address, and more specifically the duplex, carries with it an abundance of expectations about privilege, luxury, and formality. Nahem's clients were also avid collectors of contemporary art, with a penchant for the provocative and subversive. Integrating the history of the space with his clients' art collection was no easy task but proved to provide for a dynamic, highly creative interior space.

Nahem found that parts of the apartment—the stairs, floors, doors, and door hardware, for example—were in good condition, as they had been exquisitely crafted and simply required some restoration. Nahem and his clients quickly realized that the biggest organizational challenge would be to maintain the classic elegance of the floor plan while modernizing the use of the space. To that effect the kitchen was enlarged to allow for casual family dining, and the small service rooms on the upper floor were combined to create larger bedrooms and bathrooms for the family, along with more ample guest bedrooms.

Nahem left much of the foyer as it was originally designed in 1929; however, the artwork installed in this space, a collaborative effort among Alveary Architecture, Nahem, his clients, and their art consultant, aggressively introduces the subversive quality that pervades throughout the duplex. The two pieces by Jeff Koons—a pair of welcoming Yorkshire terriers, a sculptural piece in polychromed wood; and "New Hoover Deluxe Shampoo Polishers," three identical domestic appliances in an acrylic case with fluorescent lights—serve as an unexpected introduction to a home once inhabited by a former first lady.

Throughout the apartment, the intention was to install important works of art in every possible space, and to accommodate this Nahem left most of the walls without color, with the exception of the living and dining rooms. He chose a deep brown lacquer for the living room walls, as he felt that the dark reflective surface would render the large space more inviting and diminish the scale. He further fractured the space by placing two custom-designed sofas back to back, creating diverse seating areas, one facing the bar and the other facing the fireplace. This gesture also left more of the walls free for art, something that was always a primary concern for the owners and an issue that Nahem often had to design around.

In the dining room, Nahem covered the walls with glistening dark brown horsehair. The furniture plan here continues to leave ample room for art, but creates a multipurpose space as opposed to a huge dining room that might only be used a few times each year. To meet this goal Nahem designed two banquettes, covered in the same horsehair as the walls, and installed them at opposing ends of the space to create various dining options. The custom cast-bronze bookshelf, of Nahem's own design and brought to life by Randy Polumbo and his team at PLANT, running along one wall further expands the usefulness of the space.

Bold, dynamic works of art share this space with exquisite furnishings and finishes. While Nahem seems to be acutely aware of the expectations this space carries, he has chosen to partially undermine them as a design strategy in order to provide his clients with something that could become their own.

Nahem largely left the entry foyer as it was originally constructed. Here an Italian entry table from the 1940s hosts a sculpture by Jeff Koons. Another Koons work was installed in the background. The dining room, with its distinctive dark brown horsehair walls and a rare Andy Warhol above the fireplace, can be seen in the distance.

In the living room, Nahem saw the walls flanking the fireplace as an opportunity to install a pair of matching cabinets. To his clients, however, the spots provided yet more floor-to-ceiling space for art. In the end Nahem's vision of fully furnished functioning and comfortable environ-ment prevailed, complete with cabinets. The clients were still able to install works by Damien Hirst, Cindy Sherman, Andy Warhol, and Richard Prince in the room.

Nahem divided the living room into two distinct areas, one around the fireplace and the other around the bar, and used two identical custom sofas placed back to back to create these areas. The four matching club chairs, with a distinctive quilting pattern, were designed by Vladimir Kagan in the late 1930s and surround a snake-skin coffee table by Evan Lobel; a work by Damien Hirst, one of his pill cabinets, occupies an important spot in the room.

Above: Nahem designed this freestanding bar, which was inspired by a Jean Royère, to both mitigate the vast proportions of the room and create a popular spot to gather. The work behind the bar was made by the artist Piotr Uklanski and is composed of a collection of headshots of actors who have portrayed Nazis in film and television.

Nahem arranged the furniture in the dining room to encourage use beyond meals at formal occasions. The bookshelves, which were designed by Nahem and include a library ladder, render the room more casual and transform it into a part-time study. The gleaming object on the rug is a sculptural work by Anish Kapoor, and the room contains other works by Richard Prince, Andy Warhol, and Ed Ruscha.

Previous spread: Nahem created a flexible dining room by including two of his custom-designed banquettes rather than a traditional dining table set. A table by André Sornay that seats six to eight is used with one of the banquettes, along with dining chairs in original leather by Eugene Schoen, while the other presides over a pair of Jean Royère tub chairs and an ottoman upholstered in sheared mink.

Above: The kitchen was reconfigured for family dining. Nahem used glass and polished stainless for the uppers to allow for greater transparency. The kitchen floor is a bold statement. Nahem thought the tile chosen was appropriate for the building, though he decided that some color in this room would make it more user-friendly. Nahem also designed the banquette, and the artist Piotr Uklanski is responsible for the graffiti on the wall above.

Opposite: An original paneled den, one of the rooms off the central entry, was designed to create a relaxing atmosphere for the family. The space includes a game table by Pierre Paulin and artwork by Andreas Gursky and Richard Prince.

In order to create bedrooms in line with contemporary needs, Nahem consolidated a few rooms into a master suite. Here, the walls are upholstered in cashmere, which is soft to both the touch and gaze. The bed and headboard are custom Nahem designs, and the plaster light in the room is by Serge Roche. A painting by John Currin hangs over the fireplace.

On the upper bedroom floor, rooms were reconfigured to allow for his-and-hers master baths. Nahem set marble panels into nickel frames to create spaces that feel appropriate to the historic building, yet modern. The bathtub is by Waterworks, and the custom vanity with glass legs is by Fox-Nahem. Both the sink and faucet on the opposite page are original to the building.

Masterfully Designed Modernist Home

Nahem was a student of interior designer and architect Joe D'Urso at the Parsons School of Design, and D'Urso had a heavy influence on him. When the opportunity arose for Nahem to design the interiors of a ground-up, oceanfront home that his onetime professor was just completing for an amateur astronomer, Nahem jumped at the opportunity. D'Urso's design included many, if not all, of the interior finishes, so Nahem's work here was governed by his desire to pay homage to and build upon his professor's original work. While Nahem may have had a light touch, his presence is felt in every room. Nahem took cues from D'Urso and concentrated on natural fibers, textiles, materials, and hues. He also focused on simple, but masterfully designed, furnishings that he believed would honor the work of his mentor.

D'Urso's design is dominated by the home's observatory, which sits atop a dynamic collection of stucco volumes and pavilions, some with flat roofs hosting observation decks, others with pitched metal-clad roofs. The pure geometry of the observatory's massive dome, coupled with the movement of the pavilions, provides the property with a playful tone that calls to mind the work of Memphis Group founder Ettore Sottsass. While the form of D'Urso's work alludes to Memphis, D'Urso's use of pure, simple materials in their natural unadorned, unaltered state ties the architecture to the natural splendor of the site while rendering it uniquely his own.

D'Urso took advantage of the magnificent views of the dunes and ocean with large, strategically placed mahogany-framed windows throughout the home. But D'Urso's particular genius led him to understand that as the daylight subsided the ocean views would disappear, and that pushed him to create views where none initially existed. The master bedroom suite, for example, overlooks a substantial shallow, walled-in pool that D'Urso designed to host koi and water lilies. This water feature became a gathering place of wild birds in the area, and proved as much a visual reminder of the spectacular site as the direct ocean views that other rooms were able to take advantage of.

Nahem's work here became, in part, homage to D'Urso. But even when Nahem is not working in a home designed by one of his most loved professors, he displays a sensitivity to and appreciation of the architecture. For this project that meant treading lightly while simultaneously celebrating the work of his master, Nahem was careful to leave interior walls adorned in the rough plaster that D'Urso had applied throughout. And because much of the interior, including the bathrooms, kitchen cabinets, and kitchen table—which, in signature D'Urso style, is an ingenious composition of a single circular column bolted into the floor to support a round top—was done by D'Urso, Nahem was able to concentrate on furnishings and the placement of the client's extensive and impressive fossil collection. This further pushed Nahem's choice of materials toward the organic and unadorned. Natural fabrics and finishes were chosen wherever possible and Nahem kept the furnishings to a minimum, focusing on a mix of mid-century American, European, and Brazilian pieces paired with custom designs like the sofa in the living room.

Initially, D'Urso planned on the master bedroom being on the upper floor, adjacent to the home's observatory. But as he was working on the structure, he and his client decided to create a lily pond at the base of the home, in a space originally intended to host the driveway and garage. Once this decision was made, a new garage was constructed away from the home, and the space that was originally planned as a garage became a natural fit for the master. Nahem installed a lounge chair by famed Brazilian architect Oscar Niemeyer in the room.

In the living room, Nahem chose iconic mid-century furnishings as an homage to his onetime professor Joe D'Urso, the home's architect. D'Urso established the interior palette through his choice of plaster and mahogany, and Nahem was happy to follow D'Urso's lead. The owner's collection of important fossils also contributed to Nahem's choice of natural, unadorned materials and furnishings.

D'Urso largely designed the kitchen. The room features a D'Urso signature table—defying gravity by being bolted to the floor and structure below. This is a device Nahem has incorporated in other projects.

Throughout the home, Nahem relies on simple furnishings and fittings, like in the bedroom, appropriate for the direction D'Urso established with the interior and exterior architecture. In the bathroom, Nahem continues with D'Urso's palette of natural materials that celebrate the home's beachside location.

Acknowledgments

Thank you to all of the editors and publications that kindly featured and supported Fox-Nahem over the years; the many talented architects we have been fortunate enough to collaborate with; the patient tradespeople, general contractors, vendors, and artisans who helped bring our ideas and concept to reality. And my deep appreciation to David Gorman, Steve Chrostowski, Lenny Vaysberg, Dianna Pedreira, Anthony Iannacci, Jeffrey Fields, Robert and Susan Downey, and the team at Abrams: Eric Himmel, Sarah Massey, Gabriel Levinson, and designers Miko McGinty and Rita Jules.

—Joe Nahem

Credits

Greenwich Village Townhouse
Architect: Steven Harris Architects LLP
General Contractor: Eurostruct
Photographer: Peter Murdock

Oceanfront Family Home
Architect: Alveary Architecture
General Contractor: Dunn Development
Photographer: Peter Murdock

West Village Townhouse
Architect: Robert A.M. Stern Architects, LLP
General Contractor: West Village
Landscape Architect: Edmund Hollander
    Landscape Architects
Photographer: Peter Murdock

Weekend Retreat
Architect: Alveary Architecture
General Contractor: Dunn Development
Photographer: Peter Murdock

Puck Penthouse
Architect: J. L. Ramirez Architect P.C.
General Contractor: PLANT
Landscape Architect: Gunn Landscape
    Architecture
Photographer: Peter Murdock

Second Home
Architect: Alveary Architecture
Photographer: Pieter Estersohn

Gramercy Park Penthouse
Initial Design Architect: Michael Haverland
    Architect
Architect of Record: Cho / Shields Studio
General Contractor: PLANT
Landscape Architect: Gunn Landscape
    Architecture
Photographer: Peter Murdock

Central Park West Landmark
Architect: Alveary Architecture
General Contractor: PLANT
Photographer: Peter Murdock

Neo-Grec Townhouse
Architect: J. L. Ramirez Architect P.C.
General Contractor: MNC + Sons
Photographer: Peter Murdock

Chelsea Penthouse
Architect: Alveary Architecture
Landscape Architect: Gunn Landscape
    Architecture
Photographer: Peter Murdock

Connecticut Reinterpreted
Architect: Alveary Architecture
General Contractor: PLANT
Photographer: Peter Murdock

A Stanford White Townhouse
Original Architect: Stanford White
Renovation Architect: Vail Associates
    Architects
Photographers: Scott Frances/OTTO
    (Pages 200–09, 212–17) and
    Laura Resen (Pages 199, 210–11)

Architecture and Design
Architect: Selldorf Architects
General Contractor: Wright & Co.
Landscape Designer: Miranda Brooks
    Landscape Design
Photographer: Peter Murdock

Storied Park Avenue Duplex
Original Architect: Rosario Candela and
    Arthur Loomis Harmon
Renovation Architect: Alveary Architecture
Photographer: Michael Moran/OTTO

Masterfully Designed Modernist Home
Architect: Joe D'Urso
Landscape Architect: Hollander Design,
    Landscape Architects
Photographer: Eric Piasecki/OTTO

Additional photography
Peter Murdock: Pages 2, 4, 6, 8, 272
Scott Frances/OTTO: Page 10
Michael Moran/OTTO: Page 268

Editor: Sarah Massey
Designer: Miko McGinty and Rita Jules
Production Manager: Anet Sirna-Bruder

Library of Congress Control Number: 2016960982

ISBN: 978-1-4197-2653-8

Printed and bound in China
10 9 8 7 6 5 4 3 2 1

Abrams books are available at special discounts when purchased
in quantity for premiums and promotions as well as fundraising or
educational use. Special editions can also be created to specification.
For details, contact specialsales@abramsbooks.com or the
address below.

ABRAMS The Art of Books
115 West 18th Street, New York, NY 10011
abramsbooks.com